The Big King

Written by Lindsey Marine
Illustrated by Judy Moffatt

Scott Foresman

I am little Will.

The King is big.

I have a little cat.

The cat is Wig.

Wig has a little hat.

The hat is on a mat.

The hat has a little house.

The house is in the hat.

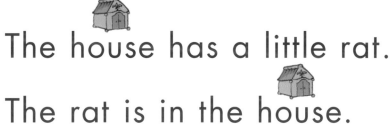

The house has a little rat.

The rat is in the house.

The rat has a watch.

The watch is big.

I have a big  watch.

I am not big.

 The king is big!